Foster's Farm

by Myka-Lynne Sokoloff
illustrated by Carol Koeller

HOUGHTON MIFFLIN HARCOURT
School Publishers

Printed in China

ISBN-13: 978-0-547-02203-1
ISBN-10: 0-547-02203-4

10 11 12 13 0940 18 17 16 15 14 13
4500443494

"Farmer Foster had a farm," sang Miss Green's class.

The children were going to visit a real farm.

"What do you think we'll see?" asked Miss Green.

Everyone was bursting with ideas.

"I think we'll see cows," said Daisy.

"I think we'll see chickens," said Alex.

"Sheep! Pigs! Goats!" said the other children.

Soon the class got to the farm.

Miss Green's children saw all kinds of surprising animals.

Alex watched a dachshund sniffing the ground.

Tony watched a tarantula crawling around its cage.

Daisy watched an iguana sunning itself on a rock.

Sam ==noticed== footprints on the muddy ground.

Soon other children were trying to match footprints with each animal's feet.

The children all thanked Farmer Foster when it was time to go. "We had a wonderful time," they said. "We want to come back next year."

Farmer Foster said, "I'm not sure we'll be open next year. We need money to care for the animals. But we don't have enough money."

The children were quiet as they climbed back onto the bus.

"How can we help the farm?" asked Miss Green. "Who has an idea to share?"

"We could record animal noises and sell CDs," said Tony.

"We could sell tee shirts!" said Sam.

The children decided tee shirts would be best.

They each made a shirt that had one of the farm animal's footprints on it.

Daisy made a shirt with dachshund footprints.

Alex made a shirt with iguana footprints.

Tony made a shirt with funny squiggles. "Iguana tail prints," he said.

Sam made a shirt with tiny dots sprinkled all over it.

"What are those dots?" asked Lisa.

"Footprints from a tap-dancing tarantula," he said.

"Very nice, Sam!" said Miss Green.

People bought all the tee shirts. They visited the farm. People told their friends. Then their friends told even more friends.

More and more people visited the farm.

That's how Foster's Farm suddenly became Foster's Famous Farm.

Responding

Story Structure

How is Farmer Foster's problem solved? Copy and complete the story map below.

<table>
<tr><td>Main Characters:
Farmer Foster, children, and Miss Green</td><td>Setting:
Foster's Farm</td></tr>
<tr><td colspan="2">Problem: Farmer Foster needs money to feed the animals and keep the farm open.
Solution: ?</td></tr>
</table>

Write About It

Text to Self Think about a time when you went somewhere with your class. Use a few sentences to tell a personal narrative about what happened. Include dialogue to show what people said.

TARGET VOCABULARY

bursting	share
noises	sprinkled
noticed	suddenly
quiet	wonderful

TARGET SKILL **Story Structure** Tell the setting, character, and plot in a story.

TARGET STRATEGY **Visualize** Picture what is happening as you read.

GENRE **Realistic fiction** is a story that could happen in real life.